BE SAFE AROUND FIRE

BRIDGET HEOS   ILLUSTRATED BY SILVIA BARONCELLI

Amicus Illustrated is published by Amicus
P.O. Box 1329, Mankato, MN 56002
www.amicuspublishing.us

Library of Congress Cataloging-in-Publication Data
Heos, Bridget.
 Be safe around fire / Bridget Heos ; illustrated by Silvia Baroncelli.
      pages cm — (Be safe!)
 Includes bibliographical references.
 Summary: "A young girl teaches her dolls, action figures, and toys the fire safety rules she has just learned in school" — Provided by publisher.
 ISBN 978-1-60753-444-0 (library binding) —
ISBN 978-1-60753-659-8 (ebook)
1. Fire prevention–Juvenile literature. 2. Fire safety engineering —Juvenile literature. I. Baroncelli, Silvia, illustrator. II. Title.
TH9148.H45 2015
613.6–dc23   2013032362

Editor: Rebecca Glaser
Designer: Kathleen Petelinsek

Printed in the United States of America,
at Corporate Graphics in North Mankato, Minn.
10 9 8 7 6 5 4 3 2 1

ABOUT THE AUTHOR

Bridget Heos is the author of more than 60 children's books, including many advice and how-to titles. She lives safely in Kansas City with her husband and four children. You can find out more about her at www.authorbridgetheos.com.

ABOUT THE ILLUSTRATOR

Silvia Baroncelli has loved to draw since she was a child. She collaborates regularly with publishers in drawing and graphic design from her home in Prato, Italy. Her best collaborators are her four nephews, daughter Ginevra, and organized husband Tommaso. Find out more about her on the web at silviabaroncelli.it

Your new house sure is dreamy. But is it safe from fires?
Well, we learned at school that the best way to stay safe is to
prevent fires. Whose sparkly shirt is that hanging on the lamp?

Super Dave, you should never put anything on a lamp! Don't cover a lamp with a blanket to make a fort or to read while in bed. Cloth can catch fire that way. So can paper.

You can't start a fire in the fireplace! Only grown-ups should use matches. They must be put away safely.

Monster babies, what should you do if you see matches lying around?

You should tell a grown-up right away. And keep younger siblings away from matches, too.

Do you have smoke alarms? Good. Test them once a month to make sure they are working.

What do you do if you hear the smoke alarm?

You can't just cover your ears! Smoke alarms are loud for a reason. They tell you there is a fire.

You must take action. You need a fire escape plan. Let's get the whole family together.

Talk about how to escape a fire in any room. Have a backup plan in case one entrance is blocked.
What if the fire is upstairs?

If Super Dave is off saving the planet, use an escape ladder. You can climb out the window if the stairs are blocked. Once you are outside, meet in one place away from the house, such as the neighbor's driveway.

That way, you will know everybody is safe. Don't go back inside for anything.

You can live without your cape. The important thing is to stay alive. Let's do the fire drill again.

Walk calmly, but quickly, to the exit. If there is a fire, get low, where it's not as smoky.

If any part of you is on fire, stop, drop and roll. That will put the fire out.

Count heads to make sure everybody made it outside.
If it's a real fire, then call 911.
(Don't call if it's just a drill!)

What if a fire alarm goes off somewhere else?
If you're at school, your teacher will lead you to
safety. Be quiet and follow ALL directions.

If you're somewhere else, know where the exits are. If you hear an alarm or smell smoke, make your way toward the exit calmly. I hope you feel safer now!

Well, safe from fire at least!

FIRE SAFETY RULES TO REMEMBER

- Never cover lamps with clothing or paper.
- Only grown-ups should use matches. Report matches or lighters left lying around to a grown-up.
- Have working smoke alarms in every bedroom.
- Have a fire escape plan at home.
- Practice the escape plan with a fire drill.
- During a school emergency, stay quiet and follow the teacher's directions.
- At a public place, know where the exits are. Stay calm in case of an emergency and make your way to an exit.

GLOSSARY WORDS

911 The emergency phone number to call for police, firefighters, and ambulances.

emergency exit The fastest way out of a building.

escape ladder A ladder that attaches to an upstairs window, allowing people to climb down the side of the house.

fire drill An exercise in which a fire alarm sounds and people practice safely exiting a house or building.

fire escape plan A plan to safely exit a house or building in case of a fire.

smoke alarm A machine that senses smoke and sets off a loud buzzing sound.

READ MORE

Kesselring, Susan. *Being Safe with Fire.* Mankato, Minn.: The Child's World, 2011.

Mara, Wil. *If there is a Fire. What Should I Do?* Ann Arbor, Mich.: Cherry Lake, 2012.

Miller, Edward. *Fireboy to the Rescue! A Fire Safety Book.* New York: Holiday House, 2009.

Pendziwol, Jean. *No Dragons for Tea.* Toronto: Kids Can Press, 1999.

WEBSITES

FIRE SAFE KIDS!
http://www.firesafekids.org/
Ask real firefighters questions and practice fire safety with fun games.

SPARKY THE FIRE DOG
http://www.sparky.org/
Learn all about fire trucks, download printable activities, and read the story of Sparky the Fire Dog.

U.S. FIRE ADMINISTRATION FOR KIDS
http://www.usfa.fema.gov/kids/flash.shtm
Read fire safety tips, play games, and quiz yourself to become a junior fire marshal.